GAY RESPECT
in the
GOOD NEWS

(still) a draft for discussion

Stephen Joseph Wolf

retired parish priest

idjc.org

A tree
gives glory to God
by being a tree.

Thomas Merton
New Seeds of Contemplation

**Gay Respect in the Good News:
(still) a draft for discussion**
Copyright © 2016, 2019 Stephen Joseph Wolf
All rights reserved.

Except where otherwise indicated, Scripture texts in this work are taken from the ***New American Bible, revised edition*** © 2010, 1991, 1986, 1970 Confraternity of Christian Doctrine, Washington, D.C. and are used by permission of the copyright owner. All Rights Reserved. No part of the New American Bible may be reproduced in any form without permission in writing from the copyright owner.

ISBN 978-1-937081-68-3

printed and distributed by Ingram
published by idjc press

Original Pocket Edition ISBN 978-1-937081-53-9
Ebook edition ISBN 978-1-937081-54-6

Rev. Steve Wolf is a retired parish priest in Nashville, who now spends more than just Mondays in silence and solitude writing for faith-sharing groups and spiritual direction.

www.idjc.org/gay_respect_in_the_good_news

1

Some years ago a good man's profession brought him to the parish where I then served as pastor. He made some friends there and became attracted to the Catholic way of giving God thanks and praise in a community of believers within the Church universal. Indeed, he became through this parish part of the one Body of Christ. He was a very happy man, though there was always a sense of something more to him.

During my next assignment this good man died, and at his funeral we all met his life partner, another good man. Two good gay men. We asked the love of his life why he had not shared with us this important part of his life story, and were told that he was a very private person.

As I prayed for and about this good gay man who had shared with me as his pastor so much of his life story, a disturbing concern kept visiting: Had I somehow put out a message that I was not a safe place for a gay man to tell his truth? Did I communicate that he was welcome in the parish as long as he stayed in the closet?

Communication is done with words, but also with words not spoken and all kinds of relatings that are part of daily human life. Had my comfort with the closet put up a wall between us? And had I let this happen with others?

These questions became a tender haunting shared at a weekday mass, after which I was so very patiently challenged about another time when I was unable to be present to a young gay man in deep pain in a way Jesus would have had me be.

It has become clear to me that my Church has not been doing what Jesus would have us do in walking the human journey of faith in God with Catholics who discover and faithfully discern whether being lesbian, gay, bisexual, transgender, intersex, or queer in any way might be part of the truth of who they are.

I heard by myself on a Monday of one of my great celibate vacations what Pope Francis said on July 29, 2013 *(footnotes begin on page 37):

> *If someone is gay*
> *and he searches for the Lord*
> *and has good will*
> *who am I to judge?*

I was in tears. Something was different, and it has taken a while to sort out just what.

In the meantime, I continued to attend PFLAG meetings as a safe place to share my story and hear stories of others and their parents and friends. Stories told and heard in confidence led me to trust more deeply in God's loving concern.

I am a reader, and one of the more helpful writings in my personal healing has been from James Alison who proposes that the world is undergoing a discovery that there is

> *a regularly occurring*
> *non-pathological*
> *minority variant*
> *in the human condition...*
> *which we currently call 'being gay.'**

As the *Catechism of the Catholic Church* calls us to journey with people who experience deep seated same-sex attractions with **respect**, **compassion**, and **sensitivity**, I propose the words of both Pope Francis and Mr. Alison for pondering within the tradition of the Church.

In this little essay, I hope to share some thoughts to Catholics who have discovered or are discerning whether *being gay* is part of what is true about them, and to their families and friends.

A pastoral encounter begins with whether this person in front of me knows of God's personal unlimited unconditional love. That is always the beginning. Always. Everything comes out of this truth. I might share a copy of *31 Days of God's Love-Call**, a collection of Old Testament readings on the love of God.

Some folks prefer to use their own Bible:
31 Days of God's Love-Call

1. Psalm 63:1-8
2. Psalm 46
3. Isaiah 55:1-13
4. Wisdom of Solomon 9:1-6,9-11
5. Psalm 23
6. Psalm 139:1-18,23-24
7. Isaiah 43:1-5a
8. Exodus 16:4-5,9,10b
9. Hosea 2:10-22
10. Psalm 131
11. Psalm 8
12. Psalm 103
13. Psalm 104
14. Psalm 19
15. 1st Kings 19:4-9a,11-13
16. Jeremiah 29:11-14
17. Ezekiel 16:4-13
18. Jeremiah 18:1-6
19. Genesis 2:4-25
20. Genesis 1:24-31
21. Isaiah 54:4-10
22. Deuteronomy 30:15-20
23. Isaiah 62:1-5
24. Ecclesiastes 3:1-11,14b
25. Psalm 62:2-10,12,13a
26. Wisdom of Solomon 11:21-12:1
27. Psalm 91:1-12,14-16
28. Ezekiel 36:24-28
29. Ezekiel 37:1-14
30. Isaiah 40:1-11
31. Psalm 130

One way to summarize these readings is my *summary of the whole Bible, taking it as a long love letter by way of revelation:

My Beloved,

I have made you in my image,
one and unique,
not like anyone ever has been
or ever will be
made in my image.

Having made you, I know you,
all the great things
your ego wants everyone to know,
those things you do not want anyone to know,
and everything you do not yet know yourself.

And in knowing you, I love you,
neither because of your strengths
nor in spite of your weaknesses;
there is nothing you can do
that will make me love you,
and there is nothing you can do
that will keep me from loving you.

Remember this always:
that I love you just is.

- God

There is an old story told about a man whose dying father begs him to promise to spend twenty minutes each day sitting silently alone in the best room of the house. In the story, that son becomes the most respected person of the town.

What does *the best room of the house* mean to you? Jesus told his disciples that they did not choose him but that he chose them and has called them friends (John 15:15b). The only way any of us becomes friends with anyone is by spending so much time together that we become happy to simply waste time with each other. This is why my favorite definition of prayer is *wasting time with God*. I beg you to choose one of those 31 passages (there's one for each day of the month), read it once or twice or thrice, choose one word or phrase or image from it, and sit with it for twenty minutes in the best room of your house.

Hear God say to you in the center of your soul, *My Beloved, I made you, I know you, and I love you.* Accept God's acceptance of you.

If our Church has failed to proclaim this truth of God's complete love for you, hear it now. Let God speak God's name in your inmost being. If Sunday Mass has not been a safe place for you, you have nevertheless known somehow in the center of your soul that God was still loving you.

Fair warning. You may yet be called by Jesus to draw on the strength that comes from the grace of God to forgive your Church. But take a breath. Please do not rush too quickly into this; give yourself room to listen for how God may call you into this grace. I myself have only been able to do so because of the grace of God, never on my own. God will give that healing grace. I can give witness to that gift. We can return to this later.

Discovering whether one is gay is not the same as discerning one's love-life vocation.

Realizing that the term *gay* is particular to recent decades, history cannot deny that there seem to have always been some minority of the world's population who discover they are gay.

It has taken a great variety of forms through the centuries and in different cultures. Its psychological genesis remains largely unexplained. (Catechism 2357)

Perhaps also largely unexplained is how from fear or homophobia or simply not knowing what to do with same-sex attraction, the spoken and unspoken message heard even in my youth was to keep this to yourself. This is private, no one else's business. Don't bother other people with it.

There is still something true about this. One's sexuality is a private personal sacred truth which is really no one else's business. However when the flip side standard is that none of this can ever be shared with anyone, this very sacred part of one's human identity can close down. It won't go away.

See the difference? A gay person's sexuality is so sacred that it is the business of no one else, until it becomes time for a gay person to have a safe way to talk about it and begin the process of discovering whether this is true about oneself.

For some, this discovery will take some time. There are many people who experience feelings of same-sex attraction who later discover themselves to be heterosexual. Many others know themselves to be gay from the first time they think about it.

So again, all need to be allowed the time it takes to let this discovery be revealed. The second need is for a safe space to talk about it. We would hope that parishes might be the logical place to find a safe person and place for opening up this questioning. Or parents. Or best friends. With regrets this is not always so. Folks who are not gay can be a huge help with clarity in this discovery.

Many of the young people in recent years discovering this truth about themselves have some things to tell my generation. Once making this discovery, staying in the closet is not healthy. I have seen the damage to the soul and psyche that can come from living decades in denial to oneself.

Here is the ***respect-compassion-sensitivity*** paragraph in the Catechism:

> The number of men and women who have deep-seated homosexual tendencies is not negligible. ~~They do not choose their homosexual condition;~~ *This inclination, which is objectively disordered constitutes* for most of them ~~it is~~ a trial. They must be accepted with **respect**, **compassion**, and **sensitivity**. Every sign of unjust discrimination in their regard should be avoided. These persons are called to fulfill God's will in their lives and, if they are Christians, to unite to the sacrifice of the Lord's Cross the difficulties they may encounter from their condition. (Catechism 2358)

Note: The *Catechism of the Catholic Church* was published in 1994, the first universal catechism in 400 years, since the Council of Trent. ~~The words stricken through were omitted~~ in *the modifications of September 8, 1997, in italics*. Modifications became necessary after Saint Pope John Paul II's teaching on the death penalty, reflected in paragraph 2267. **Bold** added.

This paragraph is packed with important messages and so is worthy of time in prayer: It seems always to have been true that some people are gay. Avoid any unjust discrimination. Gay Christians are still Christians, still part of the Church. People who are gay are to be accepted, and respected, and with sensitivity to be "com-passioned" (suffered-with).

Many Catholics who are gay have felt judged by their Church, especially in the last couple of decades. Is it not strange to hear a Pope ask, *Who am I to judge?* How many Catholics must have asked, *If not you, who? Did Jesus not give you the keys to the kingdom?* This is a reasonable question, perhaps one of those great questions that can lead us into good prayer-pondering.

I do not feel qualified to answer this question for Pope Francis, but my prayer-pondering in the Year of Mercy kept taking me to another place in the Catechism:

> Man has the right to act in conscience and in freedom so as personally to make moral decisions. *He must not be forced to act contrary to his conscience. Nor must he be prevented from acting according to his conscience, especially in religious matters.* (Catechism 1782)

The second sentence, in italics, is from the Vatican II document *Dignitatis Humanae, Declaration on Religious Liberty* of December 7, 1965, fifty years ago. Throughout that document can be found a *just requirements of public order* exception, which is to say that freedom of conscience and religious liberty do not allow me to cause harm to others.

Saint John Henry Cardinal Newman called conscience the *aboriginal Vicar of Christ*. Following one's conscience is not permission to do as one pleases. A better way to think of conscience is as our taskmaster, or again from Vatican II *Gaudium et Spes* found in the Catechism:

> *Deep within her conscience the human discovers a law which she has not laid upon herself but which she must obey. It's voice, ever calling her to love and to do what is good and to avoid evil, sounds in her heart at the right moment... For the human has in her heart a law inscribed by God... Her conscience is the human's most secret core and her sanctuary. There she is alone with God whose voice echoes in her depths.*
>
> (Catechism 1776)

You might be surprised to hear how controversial this teaching has become, though perhaps it has always been so. Some go so far as to say that your conscience must agree with Church teaching before you are free to act on it. And some imply no need to listen to the teaching of the Church.

You will not find me resolving this controversy. My experience has been that almost always when I am in turmoil about a moral question, pondering the Church tradition leads me to peaceful understanding. We are asked to keep drinking from the deposit of faith, even when in turmoil. For to act on conscience is to be free in the way the saints understand freedom, as the grace to be able to say only "yes" to God.

The Church is truly wise, and ignoring her wise teachings can get us into unnecessary trouble. So we grow up learning those teachings that our conscience may be as well-formed as possible in preparation for when we will be called to make tough decisions. And we make mistakes along the way; we also learn from them.

As a student of history it seems to me that some Church teachings have been from time to time both correct and incomplete.* There is a difference between the deposit of faith, which does not change, and the way the deposit of faith is articulated, which has developed in history. Perhaps this is why conscience is so vital.

The question of conscience will become vital to most Christians who discover themselves to be gay. There is simply no way around it.

Indeed many Christians who discover they are gay will study the Church's teachings as presented in the Catechism and recognize assent to it in conscience. This can be the case especially for those who also discover that they have been given the gift of celibacy. Most human beings are called to couple, but not all. The world has always needed a good number of people in the generous single vocation. Some of them have always been gay, but by no means all.

Now the *chastity* paragraph in the Catechism:

> Homosexual persons are called to chastity. By virtues of self-mastery that teach them inner freedom, at times by the support of disinterested friendship, by prayer and sacramental grace, they can and should gradually and resolutely approach Christian perfection.
>
> (Catechism 2359)

All Christians are called to chastity, which simply means being faithful in one's state of life, whether married or unmarried. What is really being said is that gay persons are called to remain unmarried. No one would expect this to not be a trial for most folks who discover themselves to be gay, but not for all, some of whom discern also the gift of celibacy. What is this gift?

To be created uniquely in the image of God means that each human person has been given by God a particular set of natural strengths and talents, some of which can be recognized as being inherited through parents and grandparents. Some talents will have a genesis that will be true but will remain largely unexplained. And we are all given in varying degrees the human virtues that all receive (fortitude, justice, prudence and temperance). Use 'em or lose 'em! And all the baptized receive the theological virtues (faith, hope and love).

Each Christian is also given one or more gifts that Saint Paul called **charisms**. (see Catechism par. 798-801) For more information on charisms, visit The Catherine of Siena Institute* (www.siena.org).

A charism, a spiritual gift, is how God the Father and God the Son through their Holy Spirit enables a person using the gift to accomplish the good God wishes to accomplish. Signs of a charism are unusually effective results when using the gift, direct or indirect feedback from others about the gift, a life-giving sense of being in God's flow, and that the gift is always for others.

Some of the charisms that show up in most every community of believers are called Lifestyle Charisms, such as Voluntary Poverty and Celibacy.

Some priests and religious receive this gift of celibacy; that makes sense. Not all who live the life of celibacy would say they have received this gift. They give witness that God's grace works in many ways that will always remain largely unexplained.

In the same way many of the lay faithful giving a free "yes" to the vocation to the generous single life have received the charism of celibacy. But not all. Many find it difficult to explain why or how they are able to live the celibate life, and many are hesitant to call it a vocation. It can be very mysterious.

I began seminary studies at the age of thirty-five, after fourteen tax seasons as an accountant and years of seasons in the single vocation. As now the basic human need for intimacy was met through the blessings of a gang of friends and a big family. Rarely was a day lonely, and I loved then as now a day by myself. Friends and family and work and volunteering at a homeless shelter kept pulling me out of myself. I did enjoy the generous single vocation.

One's "love-life" vocation is rooted in the way one has been wired by God when created in God's own image, the form of life in which one can best love and be loved. For most this will be a lifelong committed relationship with one other in marriage. For some this will be a committed religious vocation. And for some it will be as a generous single person in the world.

If there is a solid theology of the vocation to the generous single life, I have not found it.* There are two sentences in the Catechism: [2231]

> Some forgo marriage in order to care for their parents or brothers and sisters, to give themselves more completely to a profession, or to serve other honorable ends.
>
> They can contribute greatly to the good of the human family.
>
> (Catechism 2231

For the Christian who discerns that his or her love-life vocation is the generous single life*, friends and family will be very important. Being a friend is not always easy. As in marriage, it often means being inconvenienced. Perhaps the best way to learn how to be a friend is to be one. Perhaps the best way to find a friend is to ask God to find one. Certainly being a real friend is to trust that only God can love us perfectly.

Just as no one else can love me in the infinite way God does, nor can I love another in that way. Making a lifelong commitment to either marriage or to celibacy as a way to love and be loved carries a daunting human burden. Saint Augustine famously wrote in his *Confessions*, "O Lord, make me chaste, but not yet."* And yet he would say a "yes" to the call to celibacy, even with his history.

Accounts of the experience of Trappist monk Thomas Merton falling in love with his nurse tell a heavy story of being led to a deeper clarity about and fidelity to his vocation as a monk. He was given time and space to sort it out.

There is a great scene in the movie *Keeping the Faith* where a mentor priest reveals to his younger that he has fallen in love about once every ten years, and that he considers these to be times of learning what his vocation was really about.

As one friend has put it, we are sexual beings from the moment of conception until two weeks after we're dead. We all live this reality *within* our vocations, seeking ever to be faithful. Just as we rely on God's faithful grace, so too is our ultimate call to trust in God's mercy.

One mentor would often say that every life commitment worth anything will involve sacrifice. Such is the nature of commitment. But to be dominated by the fraudulent fear that forces one to never commit to anything is to barely be alive.

What I am trying to get at is how the life of celibacy might seem fearful. I get that. But if you have discovered yourself to be gay, please give some prayerful consideration to the possibility that celibacy may be the way God is calling you to love and be loved. Others have happily done so, and others are happily doing so.

When a young person discovers he or she is gay, the Church's call to be chaste is exactly the same as the call to chastity for all his or her friends and classmates. The wise know that sexual activity is best reserved for marriage. No kidding.

What about an adult making this discovery? The call to chastity is still there, but the vocation of celibacy cannot be forced because no vocation can be forced. A true vocation calls for a free yes.

Indeed many of the Christians who discover they are gay also discover they are not wired by God for the generous single vocation but for a lifelong committed relationship that may look a lot like marriage. And many of these have grown up Catholic and studied the teaching of the Church, and following their conscience discern a call into a lifelong committed relationship with a beloved of the same sex. And in obedience to conscience many of them still feel called by the Lord to practice their faith as Catholics.

And here we come to the words of **Sacred Scripture** in the Catechism:

> Basing itself on Sacred Scripture, which presents homosexual acts as acts of grave depravity, tradition has always declared that *homosexual acts are intrinsically disordered*. They are contrary to the natural law. They close the sexual act to the gift of life. They do not proceed from a genuine affective and sexual complementarity. Under no circumstances can they be approved. (paragraph 2357)

This paragraph footnotes four passages of Sacred Scripture. If one begins with the presumption that homosexual acts are grave depravity, then the passages may support this. But many who have made the discovery of being gay as part of the truth of how they have been created by God have additional insights to offer.

The four passages footnoted are Genesis 19:1-29 (the story of threatened gang rape of visitors welcomed by Lot in the town of Sodom, which the prophet Ezekiel [in 16:49] gives as an example of failing in the Hebrew ethic of hospitality and lack of charity to the poor and needy), Romans 1:24-27 (with the example of people giving up relations with people of the opposite sex for relations with people of the same sex), 1st Corinthians 6:10 (6:9 speaking of boy prostitutes and adult men who abused them, probably as part of pagan temple rituals), and 1st Timothy 1:10 (the same adult men listed here with people who are *lawless, unruly, godless, sinful, unholy, profane, killers of their fathers or mothers, murderers, the unchaste,... slave-dealers, liars, perjurers...*)

The good Christians I have met who have discovered that they are gay would agree that gang rape is wrong. Many have never had heterosexual intimacy to "give up." They agree that child sexual abuse is evil. And as one father of a lesbian daughter put it, "If someone wants to call my daughter any of those other names in 1st Timothy, I will have other words for him."

None of these passages say anything about two people of the same sex making a commitment of fidelity to each other for the rest of their lives.

There are two more verses from Sacred Scripture: Leviticus 18:22, *You shall not lie with a male as with a woman; such a thing is an abomination*; and 20:13, *If a man lies with a male as with a woman, they have committed an abomination*, the second verse also calling for the death penalty.

Those two verses work just fine for a married man who is heterosexual. When a man discovers he is part of the regularly occurring non-pathological minority variant in the human condition known in our time as being gay, not so much.

Here are literal word-by-word translations of the Hebrew in Leviticus 18:22 and 20:13*:

man not you-lie-with ones-who-lie-of woman...
man who he-lies with man lyings-of woman...

If I have already decided that same-sex attraction is unnatural, then our historical translations work just fine. Indeed they already work just fine for a man who is heterosexual.

But if I render these verses within the context of the call to the married man to be faithful to his wife, would these translations also work?

Man, lie not with a man who lies with a woman...

If a man lies with a man who lies with a woman...

Would two gay men in a lifelong committed relationship faithful to each other, neither of whom lie with a woman, be violating these two verses? In any case, they are two vague verses.

Again, these are some of the comments that I have heard from faithful gay Christians. While they may not be acceptable or agreeable to other faithful Christians, I would hesitate to dismiss them as unreasonable, or even as relativism.

I have not yet met the person who chose to be gay, though there may be people who have discovered themselves to be bisexual who have fallen in love with someone of the same sex. But gay folks have described discerning that being gay is part of how they have been created in God's image. Gay folks testify that being gay is part of their nature, and that to act as if they were not gay would be contrary to natural law.

The discovery that one is gay comes with real grieving that one will not be a parent, though some folks discover this truth after having become parents. This same grief is shared by married men and women who for whatever reason discover they cannot generate children of their own. Those who nevertheless adopt or live alive as aunts and uncles, teachers, coaches and mentors give witness to being generative in other life-giving ways.

Indeed, who in human history has been more life-giving than the unmarried Jesus of Nazareth? In perhaps a moment of introspection after his challenging teaching on marriage (he's for it) and divorce (he's against it), when his disciples say, *then it is better not to marry*, Jesus answers,

> Not all can accept [this] word,**
> but only those to whom that is granted.
> Some are *incapable of marriage* (literally *eunuchs*)
> because they were born so;
> some, because they were made so by others;
> some, because they have *renounced marriage*
> (literally *made themselves eunuchs*)
> for the sake of the kingdom of heaven.
> Whoever can accept this ought to accept it.

**The footnote to Matthew 19:11 says the *word* is probably the disciples' suggestion about celibacy, but it could also be Jesus' teaching about marriage. In any case, no Christian is intended to be a eunuch, as all share in Jesus' life-giving mission. And there are many ways God calls us to give life.

That basic human desire to be generative led me to be through Big Brothers Big Sisters* a brother to James as he grew from age eleven to age nineteen. I was not his father or priest or teacher or uncle. We became and remain brothers.

Children are indeed a blessed grace of sexual complementarity* in the sacrament of marriage, but not the only one. One gay couple tells how the complementarity of their personalities is both a gift and a challenge in their genuine affective complementarity in a way that has led friends and family to joke, "Yep; they're married."

One happy gay man has pondered how much of the disgust thrown his way reminds him of his own adolescent shock over the realization that his parents had shared sexual intimacy. He is also at a loss as to why people finding out he is gay presume automatically that he is being sexually active, a presumption that is not made when one meets an unmarried heterosexual.

Life has taught many who have seen sex as a toy or a simple energy release how temporary is the pleasure or the release. Few would seriously argue that being promiscuous* is the *ordered* use of sexuality that God intends. But some who have discovered they are gay and have an above average sex drive feel that if they cannot make a public lifelong commitment consistent with the truth that they are gay may find themselves at greater risk of random hookups. A heterosexual with a strong sex drive can *order* it toward at least the possibility of the sacrament of marriage.

One friend contends that sex is God's best joke. Another friend attended a wedding where the guests were given matchbooks with a quote from Saint Paul, *It is better to marry than to burn.* Sometimes humor tells a truth. The quote is from 1st Corinthians 7:8,9: *Now to the unmarried and to widows, I say: it is a good thing for them to remain as they are, as I do, but if they cannot exercise self-control they should marry, for it is better to marry than to be on fire.*

Paul's understanding of the human condition shows up in another verse, 1st Corinthians 7:36: *If anyone thinks he is behaving improperly toward his virgin, and if a critical moment has come and so it has to be, let him do as he wishes. He is committing no sin; let them get married.*

Evangelical writer Justin Lee adds, "After all, seeing that Adam was alone, God did not simply say, 'I am sufficient for you'; nor did God expect Adam to meet those needs with a *friend.*"*

Gay marriage became an issue in the 2004 U.S. election after Vermont began to recognize same-sex civil unions. I remember well a conversation among parish staff during which I became convinced from what I know about the U.S. Constitution that if the Catholic Church could say OK to civil unions then that would become the law of the land, but that if we did not accept civil unions then at some point same-sex marriage would become the law of the land. I did not expect it to happen so quickly.

Without saying that same-sex marriage is to be accepted, in *The Joy of Love* Pope Francis offers a *logic of integration* when dealing with *the complexity of various situations*:

> It is a matter of reaching out to everyone, of needing to help each person find his or her proper way of participating in the ecclesial community and thus to experience being touched by an "unmerited, unconditional, and gratuitous" mercy. No one can be condemned forever, because that is not the logic of the Gospel! **Here I am not speaking only of the divorced and remarried, but of everyone, in whatever situation they find themselves.** Naturally, if someone flaunts an objective sin as if it were part of the Christian ideal, or wants to impose something other than what the Church teaches, he or she can in no way presume to teach or preach to others; this is a case of something which separates from the community (cf. Mt 18:17). Such a person needs to listen once more to the Gospel message and its call to conversion. Yet **even for that person there can be some way of taking part in the life of**

> **community, whether in social service, prayer meetings, or another way that his or her own initiative, together with the discernment of the parish priest, may suggest.** (The Joy of Love, 297)

To hold up a teaching as a *fuller ideal* (The Joy of Love 307) will usually leave someone feeling judged. This has always been the case when members of the Body of Christ have been called by God in their conscience to propose that a particular correct teaching of the Church may still be incomplete. So hear some good news from Pope Francis:

> Because of forms of conditioning and mitigating factors, it is possible that in an objective situation of sin - which may not be subjectively culpable, or fully such - a person can be living in God's grace, can love and can also grow in the life of grace and charity, while receiving the Church's help to this end.
> (The Joy of Love, 305)

And he quotes himself in a footnote:

> In certain cases, this can include the help of the sacraments. Hence, *I want to remind priests that the confessional must not be a torture chamber, but rather an encounter with the Lord's mercy.*

> I would also point out that the Eucharist *is not a prize for the perfect, but a powerful medicine and nourishment for the weak.* (The Joy of the Gospel, 44,47)

the trans question

Folks who discover that they are transgender can justly expect an accompanying Church. This discovery and discernment can be especially heart-wrenching in youth. Unknowing fear has made the transgender dialogue about school bathrooms.

If one of my nieces told me that she was uncomfortable because a boy was in the girls' bathroom, I would tell her that if it was indeed a boy it would be reasonable for her to report that to a teacher. If however she was uncomfortable because a trans girl was in the girls' bathroom, I would tell her something else:

- Sometimes babies are born with confusing genitalia and sometimes when doctors and parents choose the baby's gender they choose incorrectly. That does not have to be anyone's fault, but sometimes it happens and there might be some things that can be done.

- Sometimes a person born with genitalia of one gender will discover that their real gender is the other, and that such a person is still a child of God, created uniquely in God's own image, and so is still her sibling in God's family to be treated with respect and dignity.

- Sometimes people are confused about their gender identity and need some time to safely sort things out.

- Sometimes we encounter people whose decisions in following their conscience seeking to do good discernment about what it means to be created in God's image might make us uncomfortable, but our discomfort does not automatically mean that we need to feel threatened or afraid.

- Any discomfort of ours does not give us the right to exclude another child of God from basic human activities such as going to church or school or to the bathroom.

- Sometimes God invites us to see our discomfort as an opportunity to talk to another and listen to the story of the other, perhaps even to be a friend.

- When I first met some trans folk at PFLAG meetings I admit to being a bit uncomfortable, and then was blessed to hear their stories and come to know them as friends.

- I have not yet met a trans sibling who gave me reason to be afraid in any way.

- And I believe God invites each of us to stand in defense of any child of God who is being bullied, even if that means accompanying a sister in transition and standing guard outside of a bathroom stall so the basic human need of putting human waste in the right place can be met for the good of all.

What is a Catholic who discovers that he or she is LGBTQ to do with all this?

If you have not yet heard ugly things said about you, you will. Sometimes they are intended to convince you to stay in or return to the closet. Sometimes they come from the way the people who love you are afraid for your happiness and health. Sometimes they are from a fear that our culture is changing too fast. Sometimes you may have to for your own safety simply leave Mass after a shaming homily, as I have. And at times the ugliness will sneak up on us. But Jesus told us and is still telling us to be not afraid.

If your LGBTQ discovery has taken you a lot of time and prayer and reflection, so might the people who love you need some time and prayer and reflection to process this new information. If it is vital that you hear your loved ones tell you that they still love you, it might be helpful to tell them so. They might not know how important that is for you right now. Even if that takes a little time, it will be worth the wait.

Jesus was very clear on not judging others, so it hurts all the more when we feel judged by others in the Church. Many have not been able to understand how language like *objectively disordered* has been hurtful, and whether the phrase *unjust discrimination* suggests that discrimination can be *just*. Many faithful employees of the Church are being outed by others as LGBTQ and then fired.

More sober Church responses could include the blessing of homes of LGBTQ households, the baptism to which Pope Francis calls us of children in these families, and helping *to establish or promote support groups for parents and family members* as suggested by the U.S. Bishops in *Always Our Children*.

As the world continues to make this discovery of a regularly occurring non-pathological minority variant in the human condition known in our time as being gay, we will all need to call on God's grace to keep from judging others who judge us. Asking for this grace can be a practical center of the Christian life.

In the gospels Jesus calls us to the most challenging tasks of
- loving our enemies, Mt 5:44
- praying for those who persecute us, Mt 5:44
- and forgiving. Mt 6:14

Bullying is always contrary to the good news of Jesus Christ, so some LGBTQ Catholics may fairly want to ask,
- Shouldn't my enemies learn to love me?
- Why can't persecutors be forced to stop?
- Is it fair to burden victims with forgiveness?

And these are reasonable questions in a worldview that seeks justice ultimately through power. But Jesus calls us to another way. The way of Jesus is the way of true peace brought about not by violent domination through laws and punishment, but the ultimate peace that comes through love.

Pope Paul VI is remembered for quoting the wise maxim, *No Peace Without Justice*. Responding to the violence of September 11, 2001, Pope John Paul II added to it: *No Peace Without Justice; No Justice Without Forgiveness*. His insight is that until someone forgives, the cycle of violence will never end. Until someone loves, enemies will only keep judging each other. The bugaboo is that for most of us loving and forgiving an enemy depend upon the grace of God. I cannot do them on my own.

However, I can choose to offer prayer for my persecutors. When someone in the Church says something ugly and judgmental about me or someone whom I care about, he or she might eventually need to be told that I am offended. If, that is, if I can speak this truth with compassion. The Church's call to respect, with compassion and sensitivity, means, if we take seriously the word *com-passion* (to *suffer-with*), that when her LGBTQ sons and daughters suffer so does the whole Body of Christ. Pastoral experience tells me that persecutors too are almost always in some kind of pain. Indeed, we all carry some kind of core-wound that we might be graced to name as our cross, the one Jesus calls us to pick up daily and carry in following him.

It is a grace to accept that as I carry my cross so does every human being. As I am in need of God's healing touch, so is every other human person, including one who is persecuting me.

One of several wise sayings that I carry with me is from Thomas Merton*:

The contemplative life must provide an area, a space of liberty, of silence, in which possibilities are allowed to surface and new choices become manifest.

Loving an enemy begins in being alone with God.

Then to pray for one's persecutor, the way Jesus calls for it, is not to pray for the healing that I might think the other ought to receive. That is just another form of judging and trying to dominate the other. For just as God alone has enough data to judge another, God alone knows the exact particular healing this persecutor needs.

And so the prayer I suggest Jesus calls us to offer looks something like this*:

Lord, *N*. is speaking words (or doing things) that I find hurtful (hateful, judging, violent).

> Like me, this one is created in your image.
> Like me, this one carries
> some kind of core-woundedness.
> Lord, I do not know what wounds
> might be causing this behavior,
> and *he/she/they* may not know either;
> but you, Lord, you know.
> And I believe you want to heal this one too.
> And that, Lord, is what I ask you to do.
> Lay onto *N.* your healing touch.
> Give *N.* the healing that you want to give
> and do not delay. Thank you, Lord.

This is not a one-time-for-all magic-spell prayer, but can become a healing way to respond to every instance of being visited by anger and hurt, just as Jesus did and does.

As the Church calls the Church to accept her sons and daughters who are gay with **respect**, **compassion**, and **sensitivity**, so are we Catholics who discover that we are gay called to accept the rest of the Church with **respect**, **compassion**, and **sensitivity**. As the Church and the world continues to make this discovery that there is a regularly occurring non-pathological minority variant in the human condition known in our time as being gay, some in the Church and in the world will suffer in this transition, and we are called to *suffer-with* (*compassion*) them, practicing the patience which can mean *long-suffering*.

Blessed Peter Faber warned us, *To dialogue with others, first you have to love them*. In the gospel economy, to pray for one's persecutors is to be open to receiving the grace that empowers one to love the persecutor and to forgive. This can create the possibility of the kind of truth-telling that Jesus did through his ministry, even while some were making plans to do him harm and others were coming to pattern their lives after his way.

All of this will call for great maturity for a Catholic who discovers that the truth about how he or she is created in the image of God includes being gay. This may seem unfair because it is. Love insists on child-like maturity.

The gospel call to come to love one's enemies and forgive by the path of praying for one's persecutors is as radical as the idea that God would so love God's creatures as to enter human history as one like us in all things but sin and allow those same creatures to put God on trial and convict and kill God to prove they are right, this God who would respond by rising from that death and coming through their fear to show God's own self and breathe the holy breath onto them saying, *Peace be with you*.

Maturity of faith is being humbly open to the possibility of being wrong while trusting in love that God is still leading me in my conscience. For, you see, the Holy Spirit is in charge of all this, and the Holy Spirit is always up to something.

As marriage is understood in the Church, the husband and the wife confer the sacrament of marriage on each other in their mutual exchange of consents to bond in permanence, fidelity, and openness to children. At a wedding we witness to what they do. Is it possible for two adults of the same sex to enter together into the sacrament of marriage by freely exchanging consents to bond in permanence, fidelity, and openness to life in the same way as a man and a woman who already know for whatever reason they will be unable to conceive a child? How will these unions come to be seen by the people of God? Will they recognize them also as domestic churches? Time will tell in the reality of those who feel called to such unions of the whole of their lives.

In the meantime can we figure out how to be respectful of all who are honestly seeking to be faithful to the will of God as God reveals it in their continuing-to-be-formed conscience, not judging, but giving the Holy Spirit room to do her thing? It is still my hope to remain hopeful.

-SJW

Church Sources

Always Our Children: *A Pastoral Message to Parents of Homosexual Children and Suggestions for Pastoral Ministers,* A Statement of the Bishops' Committee on Marriage and Family, United States Conference of Catholic Bishops, September 10, 1997

Catechism of the Catholic Church,
English translation for the United States of America copyright © 1994, United States Conference of Catholic Bishops
—Libreria Editrice Vaticana.

English translation of the *Catechism of the Catholic Church:* **Modifications** *from the Editio Typica* copyright © 1997, United States Conference of Catholic Bishops —Libreria Editrice Vaticana.

Paragraphs on **same-sex attraction**: 2357-2359

Paragraphs on **conscience**: 1782, 1776

Paragraphs on **charisms**: 798-801

Paragraph on **being single**: 2231

Pope Francis, ***The Joy of Love*** **(*Amoris Laetitia*),** Post-Synodal Apostolic Exhortation, *To Bishops, Priests, and Deacons, Consecrated Persons, Christian Married Couples, and all the Lay Faithful on Love in the Family,* Copyright © 2016.

***The Joy of the Gospel* (*Evangelii Gaudium*)**
2014 Libreria Editrice Vaticana, 00120, Citta del Vaticano. All rights reserved.

Other Sources

Page 2: *If someone is gay and searches for the Lord.*
and he searches for the Lord and has good will
who am I to judge?
I wrote it down the next day and still carry it with me.

Page 3: *a regularly occurring non-pathological*
minority variant in the human condition...
which we currently call 'being gay.'
The Fulcrum of Discovery or: how the gay thing is good news for the Catholic Church,
copyright © 2009 James Alison.
http://www.jamesalison.co.uk/texts/eng59.html
He uses the intriguing analogy of mapmakers after the discovery of the Americas.

Pages 3-5: **31 Days of God's Love-Call**,
copyright © 2013 Stephen Joseph Wolf, idjc press.
It is also the first chapter in **A Jesus Breviary**,
copyright © 2015 Stephen Joseph Wolf, idjc press.

Page 12: *some Church teachings have been from time to time both correct and incomplete...*;
One example is mentioned on page 9, how the way the Church articulates her teaching on the use of the death penalty had to be modified following paragraph 56 of Pope John Paul II's encyclical **The Gospel of Life (Evangelium Vitae)**, March 25, 1995. Another example is how the Church's teaching on slavery shifted very gradually from normative, to toleration, to a violation of the seventh commandment against stealing.   (Cat. 2414)

Thomas Bokenkotter shares a note from *The Tablet* (December 12, 1998) in his 2004 expanded revision of **A Concise History of the Catholic Church** (Image Books, pages 487-88) that a statement dated June 20, 1866 was signed by Pope Pius IX saying:

> *it is not contrary to the natural or divine law for a slave to be sold, bought, exchanged, or given, provided in the sale purchase, exchange or gift, the due conditions are strictly observed which the approved authors describe and explain.*   Pope Pius IX, 1866

Page 14: *The Catherine of Siena Institute at* **www.siena.org***;* Affiliated with the Western Dominican Province, the Catherine of Siena Institute is doing groundbreaking work in rediscovering the Church's long tradition on the understanding of charisms. If you can't attend one of their **Called and Gifted Workshops**, get their *Called and Gifted Complete Materials for Individuals* which includes CD's and workbooks.

Page 15: *...theology of the vocation to the..single life...*; Pope Francis does quote the 2015 Synod of Bishops' *Relatio Finalis* in *The Joy of Love* (2016):

> *Many people who are unmarried are not only devoted to their own family but often render great service in their group of friends, in the Church community, and in their professional lives. Sometimes their presence and contributions are overlooked causing in them a sense of isolation. Many put their talents at the service of the Christian community through charity and volunteer work. Others remain unmarried because they*

> *consecrate their lives to the love of Christ and neighbor. Their dedication greatly enriches the family, the Church, and society.* (The Joy of Love, 158)

Page 16: *..the generous single life, friends...*;
See the great friendship chapter in C.S. Lewis' **The Four Loves** (affection, friendship, eros, and charity), 1960.

Page 16: *O Lord, make me chaste, but not yet.*
Saint Augustine of Hippo, **Confessions**, c. 400 AD, from the Oxford University Press 1991 edition translated by Henry Chadwick, Book 8, paragraph 17:

> *I was an unhappy young man, wretched as at the beginning of my adolescence when I prayed you for chastity and said, 'Grant me chastity and continence, but not yet.' I was afraid you might hear my prayer quickly, and that you might too rapidly heal me of the disease of lust which I preferred to satisfy rather than suppress.*

Page 20: *literal word-by-word translations...in Leviticus*;
The Interlinear NIV Hebrew-English Old Testament, by John R. Kohlenberger III, copyright © 1979, 1980, 1982, 1985, 1987 Zondervan Publishing House, Grand Rapids, pages 325, 330.

Page 22: *Big Brothers Big Sisters*;
There are many children waiting on waiting lists all over our great nation for big brothers and big sisters. Since God wanted me to share in this gift, God found the time for James in the full schedule of a parish priest. And I am a better man for it.

Page 23: ...*sexual complementarity*...;
My favorite chapter on sexuality is Chapter 9 of ***The Holy Longing: the Search for a Christian Spirituality***, by Ronald Rolheiser, copyright © 1999, Doubleday, especially his beautiful litany of *sexuality in its full bloom* on page 197.

Page 23: ...*being promiscuous*...;
In ***Hidden Voices: Reflections of a Gay Catholic Priest***, copyright © 2012, my friend Gary M. Meier quotes Austrian Cardinal Christopher Schonborn saying in 2010 as have many parents and friends of LGBT Catholics,

> *We should give more consideration to the quality of homosexual relationships. A stable relationship is certainly better than if someone chooses to be promiscuous.*

Page 24: ***Torn: Rescuing the Gospel from the Gays-vs.-Christians Debate***, copyright © 2012 Justin Lee, Jericho Books. Written from an Evangelical perspective with honesty and humor, Catholics will welcome the clarity of his story and his invitation to dialogue.

Page 32: *The contemplative life must provide an area*...;
The Intimate Merton: his life from his journals, by Thomas Merton, November 7, 1968, edited by Patrick Hart and Jonathan Montaldo, Harper Collins, copyright © 1999 Merton Legacy Trust, page 351.

Page 32: *Lord, N. is speaking words (or doing things)...*;
I offer another form of this prayer for when anger is involved from ***Anger the Jesus Way: reflections on the story of Jesus healing a man with a withered hand found in Mark 3:1-6***, copyright © 2016 Stephen Joseph Wolf, IDJC press, page 13:

**Lord my God, it has happened again
and anger is visiting me.**

**I hear your gospel call to love enemies,
to pray for persecutors, and to forgive.
Because I trust in your way I pray:**

**I am angry right now with *N*.
Judging is your job alone
for you alone have all the data.
Like me, *N*. is created in your image
and loved by you without limit.
But there seems to be
something unhealed in *N*.**

**I know not what it is,
and *N*. may not know;
but you, Lord, you know:
and I believe that you want to heal it.**

**This I ask you to do.
Lay onto *N*. your healing touch.
Amen.**

For More

Building a Bridge: How the Catholic Church and the LGBT Community Can Enter Into a Relationship of Respect, Compassion, and Sensitivity,
James Martin, SJ, Harper Collins, June 13, 2017

The Inner Voice of Love: A Journey Through Anguish to Freedom, by Henri Nouwen, 1996, Doubleday. I kept copies of this book in my office to give to people in pain.

Catholic Teaching on Homosexuality: New Paths to Understanding, by Rev. Louis J. Cameli, (one of my great teachers) Ave Maria Press, 2012.

Coming Out Within: Stages of Spiritual Awakening for Lesbians and Gay Men, copyright © 1992 Craig O'Neill & Kathleen Ritter, Harper Collins.

Faith Beyond Resentment: Fragments Catholic and Gay, copyright © 2001 James Alison, The Crossroad Publishing Company.

Homosexuality and the Bible, by Walter Wink, updated in 2005, The Fellowship of Reconciliation, 16 pages, www.forusa.org.

The Rainbow Kingdom: Christianity and the Homosexual Reconciled, copyright © 2006 by fellow Clarksvillian David W. Shelton.

New Seeds of Contemplation, Thomas Merton, copyright © 1961 by the Abbey of Gethsemani, Inc., New Directions Books.

THE GOOD NEWS   43

Be not overwhelmed by these **support** opportunities but do give them each a good spare time look-see.

Courage   **www.couragerc.org**
Their five goals are chastity, prayer and dedication, fellowship, support, and good example. If someone is addicted to sex, then sexaholics anonymous or sex addicts anonymous would probably be more appropriate. And yet Courage has helped many who are called to celibacy.

Fortunate Families   **www.fortunatefamiliescom**
Catholic parents of LGBT sons and daughters sharing with others on the same journey a message of hope and **unconditional** love for their families and respect, friendship and justice for their children.

DignityUSA   **www.dignityusa.org**
Education, advocacy, and support.

New Ways Ministry   **www.newwaysministry.org**
Advocacy, research, publications, education & a blog.

Equally Blessed   **www.eqully-blessed.org**
Faithful Catholics committed to full equality.

PFLAG   **www.pflag.org**
PFLAG's roots as *parents and friends of lesbians and gays* are traced to the New York City 1972 Christopher Street Liberation Day March, when Jeanne Manford carried a sign reading **Parents of Gays: Unite In Support For Our Children** as her son Morty walked beside her. Today, the gold-standard advocated by PFLAG parents and families – and set forth by pediatricians and therapists – is to accept and support LGBTQ people's sexual orientation and/or gender identity and expression; **parental rejection is widely understood to be abusive and damaging.**

www.ingramcontent.com/pod-product-compliance
Lightning Source LLC
Chambersburg PA
CBHW052127110526
44592CB00013B/1788

*9 7 8 1 9 3 7 0 8 1 6 8 3 *